C000091172

DISCERNMENT
SERIES

DISCERNING
OF
SPIRITS

UNMASKING
THE ENEMIES
OF THE CHURCH

Truths compiled
from the writings of

FRANCIS
FRANGIPANE

Scripture taken from the New American Standard Bible
© 1960, 1962, 1963, 1968, 1971, 1972, 1973, 1975, 1977
by the Lockman Foundation. Used by permission.

ISBN # 978-0-9629049-7-4

CONTENTS

Introduction 5

1. The Gift of Discernment........................... 7

2. Eliminating False Discernment 13

3. Discerning the Nature of the Enemy 18

4. The Stronghold of Christ's Likeness 22

chapters from *The Three Battlegrounds*

INTRODUCTION

As we have served the Lord over these years, it has been our experience that the church of Jesus Christ exercises little maturity in the matter of spiritual discernment. Indeed, much of what is called discernment does not liberate the church, but sows suspicion, fear and accusation among the people.

Therefore, in this study we have sought to lay a foundation for the saints to receive the true gift of discernment. Recognizing that we, too, are still learning, we realize this study is by no means exhaustive. Ultimately, we hope to provide a more detailed manual on the gift of spiritual discernment. In the meantime, this attempt will be a necessary primer for that which is to come.

1.

THE GIFT OF DISCERNMENT

Besides speaking through the Scriptures themselves, the Holy Spirit speaks in dreams, visions, and prophetic words. But much of what is revealed will actually come through our capacity to perceive correctly. The Scriptures tell us that Jesus perceived the thoughts of men "in His Spirit." So also with us, if we are to move in divine discernment, our view of life must be purged of human thoughts and reactions.

To Discern, You Cannot Judge

The beginning of true discernment will not come until we crucify our instinct to judge. This may take many months, or even years, of uprooting all thought-systems that have not been planted in the divine soil of faith and love for people. To appropriate the discernment that is in the **"mind of Christ"** (1 Cor 2:16), we must first find the heart of Christ. The heart and love of Jesus is summed up in His own words: **"I did not come to judge the world, but to save the world"** (John 12:47).

Spiritual discernment is the grace to see into the unseen. It is a gift *of the Spirit* to perceive what is *in the spirit*. Its purpose is to see into the nature of that which is veiled. But the first veil that must be removed is the veil over our own hearts. Jesus demands we understand our own need of His mercy so that, out of the grace we have received, we can compassionately minister to others. In this process, we will discover the depravity and selfishness of our carnal nature. We will know thoroughly that the gift of discernment is not a faculty of our minds.

We must ever be conscious that Christ's goal is to save, not judge. We are called to navigate the narrow and well-hidden path into the true nature of human need. If we are to truly help men, we must remember we are following a Lamb.

This foundation must be laid correctly, for if you have discernment, you cannot react. To perceive, you must make yourself blind to what seems apparent. People may react to you, but you cannot react to them. You must always remain forgiving in nature, for the demons you cast out may speak to you in the person's voice, masquerading as the individual himself. For this very reason Jesus said, **"whoever shall speak a word against the Son of Man, it shall be forgiven him"** (Matt 12:32). Jesus was prepared in His heart to forgive men *before* they ever sinned against Him. *He knew His mission was to die for men, not condemn them.*

We are not only called into Christ's life, but into His mission as well. Jesus said, **"As Thou didst send Me into the world, I also have sent them"** (John 17:18). We are called to die that others may live. Therefore, we must realize that before our perception develops, our love must develop until our normal attitude is one of forgiveness. If God will show us the hearts of men and use us to release them from captivity, we cannot react to what they say. As our perception becomes more like that of Christ Himself and men's hearts are revealed to us, we cannot even react to what they *think*.

If we do not move in divine forgiveness, we will walk in much deception. We will presume we have discernment when, in truth, we are seeing through the veil of a "critical spirit." We must know our weaknesses, for if we are blind to our sins, what we assume we discern in men will merely be the reflection of ourselves. Indeed, if we do not move in love, we will actually become a menace to the body of Christ.

This is exactly what Jesus taught when He said,

> **"Do not judge lest you be judged. For in the way you judge, you will be judged; and by your standard of measure, it will be measured to you. And why do you look at the speck that is in your brother's eye, but do not notice the log that is in your own eye? Or how can you say to your brother, 'Let me take the speck out of your eye,' and behold, the log is in your own eye? You hypocrite, first take the log out of your own eye, and then you will see clearly enough to take the speck out of your brother's eye"** (Matt 7:1-5).

Repentance is the removal of the "logs" within our vision; *it is the true beginning of seeing clearly.* There are many who suppose they are receiving the Lord's discernment concerning one thing or another. Perhaps in some things they are; only God knows. But many are simply judging others and calling it discernment. Jesus *commanded* us to judge not. The same Eternal Hand that wrote the Law on stones in the Old Covenant is writing the Law of the Kingdom on tablets of flesh today. This word to **"judge not"** (KJV) is just as immutably final as His Ten Commandments. It is still God speaking.

The Goal is to See Clearly

The judgmental carnal mind always sees the image of itself in others. Without realizing it is seeing itself, it assumes it is perceiving others. Jesus refers to the person who judges as a **"hypocrite."** The Lord is not saying we should totally stop thinking about people. He wants us to be able to help one another. The emphasis in Jesus' command to **"judge not"** is summarized in His concluding remark: **"First take the log out of your own eye, and THEN you will see clearly enough to take the speck out of your brother's eye."** The way we help is not by judging, but by *seeing clearly!* And we do not see clearly until we have been through deep and thorough repentance— until the instinct to judge after the flesh is uprooted!

We have seen that Jesus paralleled speaking to people about their sins with taking specks out of their eyes. The eye is the most tender and sensitive part of the human body. How do you take a speck out of someone's eye? Very carefully! You must first win their trust. This entails consistently demonstrating an attitude that does not judge or instinctively condemn.

To summarize: We must see clearly to help others. We must be able to see where a person's vision is obstructed, develop trust in our relationship with them and, only then, remove their **"speck"** without judging or condemning them.

If you seek to have a heart that does not condemn and if you truly crucify your instinct to judge, you will have laid a true foundation for the gift of discernment. Your heart will then be prepared to receive dreams, visions, and insights from God. You will be unstained by human bias and corruption.

2.

ELIMINATING FALSE DISCERNMENT

If what you have to say to someone is very important, you ask for their undivided attention. So also God does not speak to us until we slow down, tune out the static of our world, and give Him our attention. To walk in true discernment, our hearts must be quiet before God. We must learn how to listen.

Cease Striving and Know

God wants us to learn how to listen and wait upon Him. We read of the Lord's command in the Psalms: **"Be still, and know that I am God"** (Ps 46:10 KJV). We cannot engage in spiritual warfare without first being conscious of God and, through Him, be discerning of the enemy. All true discernment comes through a heart that has ceased striving, a heart that knows, even in the fiery trial of its personal struggle, that the Lord is God.

There is a "jamming station" that inhibits our powers of discernment. Our *thoughts* and *reactions* block us from hearing God. Until the motor of the carnal mind is turned off, true discernment will not consistently be ours. We must die to personal judgments, ideas of retaliation, and self-motivation. Indeed, Jesus said, **"I can do nothing on My own initiative. As I hear, I judge"** (John 5:30). He ceased striving. We also must learn to *listen* to the voice of the Holy Spirit. As we stop our striving, *as we hear*, we discern.

Abounding Love Brings Discernment with It

"And this I pray, that your love may abound still more and more in real knowledge and all discernment" (Phil 1:9). Discernment comes from abounding love. What is abounding love? It is love that leaps out from us toward others. It is motivated by long-term commitment; it is anointed by sacrificial charity.

There is a false discernment that is based on mistrust, suspicion, and fear. You can recognize false discernment by the coldness around it. False discernment may be packaged in a type of love, but it does not originate in love; it comes out of criticism. True discernment is rooted deeply in love.

Picture, if you will, a long-haired young man. His clothes are unkempt and he has tattoos on his arms. It is night, and he is walking toward you on a lonely street. It is easy to judge such a person after the obvious and superficial. Yet, look at this young man in the same setting, but through his mother's eyes. From this perspective, his outer appearance is less threatening; you have insight into his life and *hope* for his future. You now see a little boy growing up without a father, a child rejected often by his friends. You have a commitment that runs deep toward this young man. It is sustained by a love that you carried throughout his life, from the pain of childbirth to suffering with him in his adolescence.

Those with false discernment see the *outside* of a person or situation and pretend they know the *inside*. Their discernment is false because they are not committed to the process of labor and birth! Godly discernment comes from godly motives; godly motives are rooted in committed love for the church.

"Do not judge according to appearance, but judge with righteous judgment" (John 7:24). Righteous judgment is the direct result of love. If you cannot pray in love for a person or the church, do not presume you have true discernment. *Love precedes peace, and peace precedes perception.* Without love and peace in your heart, your judgment will be overly harsh. Regardless of the smile upon your face, your heart will have too much anger. False discernment is always slow to hear, quick to speak, and quick to anger.

Peace Must Rule Our Hearts

There is a tension underlying false discernment, an anxiety that pressures the mind to make a judgment. True discernment emerges out of a tranquil and pure heart, one that is almost surprised by the wisdom and grace in the voice of God. Remember, our thoughts will always be colored by the attitudes of our hearts. Jesus said, **"Out of the abundance of the heart the mouth speaketh"** (Matt 12:34 KJV). He also said, **"out of the heart of men, proceed the evil thoughts"** (Mark 7:21). Again He said, **"the pure in heart . . . shall see God"** (Matt 5:8). From the heart the mouth speaks, the eyes see, and the mind thinks. In fact, Proverbs 4:23 (KJV) tells us that **"out of it** [the heart] **are the issues of life."**

Our perception of life is based upon the condition of our heart. This is vital because the gifts of the Spirit must pass through our hearts before they are presented to the world around us, and if our hearts are not right, the gifts will not be right, either.

When our heart has unrest we cannot hear from God. Therefore, we must learn to *mistrust* our judgment when our heart is bitter, angry, ambitious, or harboring strife for any reason. The Scripture tells us to allow **"the peace of Christ** [to] **rule** [act as arbiter] **in your hearts"** (Col 3:15). To hear clearly from God, we must first have peace.

Solomon wrote, **"One hand full of rest is better than two fists full of labor and striving after wind"** (Eccl 4:6). There is too much labor and toil in our minds, too much striving after the wind. If we want discernment we must become aggressively calm. This is not a passive state of mind, but an expectant, focused, waiting upon God. Discernment comes from our sensitivity to Christ in the realm of the Spirit. It comes from love as our motivation, peace in our hearts, and a poised and waiting attitude of mind toward God. Through a life so prepared by God, the gift of discernment is revealed.

3.

DISCERNING THE NATURE OF THE ENEMY

The Lord is raising up an army, uniting His people, equipping them, and preparing them to take their cities.

Hitting the Heart of Your Adversary

In the spirit realm the *name* of an entity always corresponds to its *nature*. You will notice that there are many names given to the Lord in Scripture. Yet, each revealed name is actually a deeper revelation of His nature (see Genesis

22:14; Exodus 3:14). Similarly, the names of the Lord's angels are also self-descriptive. This principle of consistency between the name and nature of spiritual beings holds true in discerning the activity and purpose of evil spirits. To defeat the rulers of darkness, we must know their nature—their tactics and how they apply those tactics against our weaknesses.

In the Bible, the term "unclean spirit" is a generic term used simply to draw a distinction between angelic spirits and evil spirits. But if you want to bring deliverance, you need to know the *nature* of a specific unclean spirit; that is, whether the unclean spirit is a spirit of fear or sexual lust, etc.. You do not need to ask it any more questions once you know its nature.

Consider that the name of the unclean spirit inhabiting the Gerasene demoniac was **"Legion"** Why? **"For we are many"** (Mark 5:6-9). Knowing the name helped Jesus discern its nature, thus facilitating the actual deliverance. When John describes the fallen angel in Revelation 9:11 as the "king" over the demons in the bottomless pit, he reveals this ruler's name **"in Hebrew is Abaddon, and in the Greek he has the name Apollyon."** In English, these names are "Destruction" and "Destroyer" respectively. Again, the name and nature match.

Once you know its nature, however, you do not need to know its name. If you were in warfare against "Abaddon," you could identify the spirit with the name "Destruction" or "Destroyer" as readily as using the Greek name "Apollyon." It's the same spirit manifested through different names. You could war against it, if God so led you, by simply calling it the spirit of destruction.

How do we defeat the enemy? Our victory begins with the name of Jesus on our lips, uttered in fervent prayer. Our triumph is consummated by the transformation of our nature, where Christ Himself dwells as Lord in our hearts.

Follow the Lamb!

We have touched on a few of the enemies of God in this study. It is very important to *not* charge ahead, attacking principalities in warfare without having strategies and without people praying for the protection of those doing warfare.

In Scripture, we have a clear picture of the proper balance in all warfare: **"the armies which are in heaven . . . were following *Him*"** (Rev 19:14). In no other dimension of life will we find the phrase "a little knowledge is a dangerous thing" more true than in spiritual warfare. The armies which are in heaven *follow*! Who do they follow? *Jesus!*

Therefore, let us be very conscious and very careful to be followers of the Lord. From our experience, it is vital that the people in your church be trained in warfare *before* laying a large-scale siege against the enemy. Your attack against the strongholds of hell will be in the areas of your knowledge. Satan, on the other hand, will counterattack in the areas of your ignorance.

It is essential we understand the difference between being taught and being *trained.* Reading this book is being taught; being personally led by the Lord Jesus is being trained. David wrote, **"He *trains* my hands for battle, so that my arms can bend a bow of bronze"** (Ps 18:34). This booklet is meant to inform you of your need for training and to provide certain insights and guidelines. What you learn in confrontational warfare and obedience to the Lord as you place your confidence in Him will far exceed that which any book can provide.

Notes

4.

THE STRONGHOLD OF CHRIST'S LIKENESS

Victory begins with the name of Jesus on our lips. It is consummated by the nature of Jesus in our hearts.

God's Highest Purpose

Most Christians only engage in spiritual warfare with a hope of either relieving present distresses or attaining a "normal" existence. However, the purpose of all aspects of spirituality, warfare included, is to bring us into the image of Christ. Nothing, neither worship, warfare, love, nor deliverance, is truly attainable if we miss the singular objective of our faith: Christlikeness.

Let us recall that the Lord delivered the ancient Hebrews *out* of Egypt in order that He could bring them *into* the Promised Land. Likewise, we are delivered *out* of sin, not that we might live for ourselves, but that we might come *into* Christlikeness. Our goals must align with God's, for if our nature does not change, we will invariably find ourselves entangled in the same problems that *caused* our difficulties in the first place.

While we may not want to hear this, many of our spiritual conflicts simply are not going to cease until the character of the Lord Jesus is formed in our hearts. The Father's goal in deliverance is much more than simply seeing our burdens or the devil taken off our backs. Indeed, the specific purpose toward which God is working all things is our conformity **"to the image of His Son"** (Rom 8:29). The Father's purpose in our salvation was that Jesus would become **"the first-born among many brethren"** (Rom 8:29). In other words, the way to realize God's ultimate victory is to reach toward His ultimate goal, which is complete transformation into the likeness of Christ.

There is a penetration of spirit between God and ourselves, where our spirits are fully saturated with the Living Presence of the Lord Jesus, where His glory so floods our lives that there is

"no dark part" left within us (Luke 11:36). This immediacy of the Lord's Presence produces an indestructible defense—a fortress within which we are hidden from evil. Through Christ, as we enter the excellence of His ways, our relationships both with the Father and with one another are lifted to a place of immunity from countless satanic attacks. Indeed, as His fullness within us increases, that which is written is fulfilled: **"as He is, so also are we in this world"** and, **"He who was born of God keeps him** [us] **and the evil one does not touch him** [us]" (1 John 4:17; 1 John 5:18).

We must realize that it is not Satan who defeats us; it is our *openness* to him. To perfectly subdue the devil we must dwell in the **"shelter of the Most High"** (Ps 91:1). The warfare between the church and the devil facilitates a purpose greater than merely the defeat of Satan. To survive the devil's assault we are forced to appropriate Christ's likeness—and this transformation of our souls is God's highest goal! Thus, the faith and love of Christ become our only place of safety.

Once we realize that the Father's goal is to transform our lives with Christ's life, we will continually find that God has one answer to spiritual warfare: *We are to appropriate the nature of His Son!* Are you troubled by demons of fear or doubt? Submit those areas to God, repenting of your unbelief, and then yield yourself to

Christ's faith within you. Are you troubled with spirits of lust and shame? Present those very areas of sin to God, repent of your old nature and draw upon the forgiveness of Christ and His purity of heart.

The Father is more concerned with the coming forth of His Son in our lives than He is in defeating Satan. Who is the devil that he can defy the Living God? Once the devil recognizes that his assault against your life has not pulled you *from* God but is causing you to run *toward* God, and once he perceives that his temptations are actually forcing you to appropriate Christ's virtue, the enemy will withdraw.

The Goal is Christlikeness, Not Warfare

There is a time when the Lord calls us to pull down the strongholds of hell over our churches and our communities. There is another time, however, when to engage in much spiritual warfare is actually a *distraction* from your obedience to God. Jesus defeated Satan at Gethsemane on the cross, not by directly confronting the devil, but by fulfilling the destiny to which He had been called. *The greatest battle that was ever won was accomplished by the apparent death of the victor, without even a word of rebuke to His adversary!* The prince of this world was judged and principalities and powers were disarmed, not by confrontational warfare, but by the surrender of Jesus Christ on the cross.

There are occasions when your battle against the devil is actually a digression from the higher purpose God has for you. Intercessors and warfare captains take note: There is a demon whose purpose is to focus one's mind on hell. If you are continually "seeing" evil spirits in people or in the material world around you, this spirit may be attempting to lure your attention away from the Lord. The ultimate goal of this demon is to produce mental illness in saints who move in the ministry of deliverance. *Listen very carefully: We are not called to focus on the battle or the devil, except where that battle hinders our immediate transformation into Christ's likeness.*

Our highest calling is to focus on Jesus. The work of the devil, however, is to draw our eyes away from Jesus. Satan's first weapon always involves distracting us from Christ. Turn to Jesus and, almost immediately, the battle vanishes.

I knew a man who owned a record company. Besides running the operation, he also spent many hours in production listening to the "mother disk," which was the record from which all subsequent records were pressed. Over the years, his ears became adept at catching the "pops and sizzles," the imperfections that had to be eliminated in the master disk. I remarked one day that I thought working with music must be enjoyable. His response was enlightening. He said, "You know, I haven't listened to music in years. When I turn on my sophisticated home stereo, no matter what recording I'm listening to, all I hear are the 'pops and sizzles.' "

In the same way his thoughts were bent toward musical imperfections, so this spirit will seek to turn your thoughts continually toward the enemy. Suddenly, all you will see are demons. The true gift called "discerning of spirits" is a balanced gift which enables you to recognize at least as many angelic spirits as you do evil spirits. The proper manifestation of this gift has a much more positive focus and influence than that which commonly masquerades as discernment.

An example of the proper balance in discernment is seen in Second Kings. The Syrian army had surrounded a city in Israel, much to the consternation of the servant of the prophet Elisha. To calm his fright, Elisha prayed that his servant's eyes would be opened. He then encouraged his servant, saying, **"Do not fear, for** *those who are with us* **are more than** *those who are with them"* (2 Kings 6:16). As the Lord opened the servant's eyes, he also saw what Elisha saw: **"the mountain was full of horses and chariots of fire all around Elisha"** (v 17).

In spiritual warfare, the battle is never a simple "us against them" human affair. It always includes **"those . . .** *with us"* against **"those . . .** *with them."* True discernment is as fully aware of the vast multitude of angels loyal to God as it is aware of the activity of the demonic realm—and it is aware that the angelic hosts on our side are both stronger and more numerous than the enemy. Remember, if you fail to "hear the music" in your times of warfare, your discernment is, at best, incomplete.

We must learn that, on a personal level, it is better to develop godly virtues than to spend our day praying against the devil. Indeed, it is the *joy of the Lord* that casts out spirits of depression. It is our *living faith* that destroys spirits of unbelief; it is *aggressive love* that casts out fear.

As we continually yield ourselves to Christ, surrendering ourselves by faith to His nature and His words, we literally build the impenetrable stronghold of His Presence around us. The way into the fortress of the Almighty is simple. ***Victory begins with the name of Jesus on our lips. It is consummated by the nature of Jesus in our hearts.***

DISCIPLESHIP TRAINING BOOKLETS

(10+ AT 40%, 100+ AT 50% DISCOUNT)

COMPILED/FORMATTED FOR GROUP STUDY BY FRANCIS FRANGIPANE

Discerning of Spirits

Chapters: The Gift of Discernment; Eliminating False Discernment; Discerning the Nature of the Enemy; The Stronghold of Christ's Likeness.

#FF1-018 $4.65

The Jezebel Spirit

Chapters: Discerning the Spirit of Jezebel; Elijah, Jehu and the War Against Jezebel; Our Experience with Jezebel; Strategy Against the Spirit of Jezebel; Free to Laugh

#FF1-019 $4.65

Prevailing Prayer

Chapters: Legal Protection; Day and Night Prayer; Sent by God; Repentance Precedes Revival; Covenant Power

#FF1-011 $4.65

Overcoming Fear!

by Denise Frangipane

Testimony & Keys to Releasing the Power of Faith.   #DF1-003 $4.65

Exposing the Accuser of the Brethren

Chapters: Exposing the Accuser; Casting Down the Accuser; Protected from the Accuser; At the Throne with God

#FF1-017 $4.65

A bestseller on how to protect yourself and prosper in the midst of battle.

A Time to Seek God

Chapters: The Tent of Meeting; Two Things, Two Things Only; Unrelenting Love; Drawing Near to the Holy God; A Place for Him to Rest; The Way into the Holy Place

#FF1-020 $3.95

Deliverance from PMS

by Denise Frangipane

Practical and Spiritual Helps Toward Deliverance from PMS.

#DF1-002 $3.95

AUDIO ALBUMS

MESSAGE OF THE MONTH ANNUAL U.S. SUBSCRIPTION IS $49.00 (PLUS $9 SHIPPING)

Please visit www.arrowbookstore.com for a complete listing.

Jezebel Spirit

#1FF5-041   6 tapes $36.00
#2FF-041 6 CDs $36.00

The War Mode

#2FF-001 4 CDs $24.00

Pulling Down Strongholds

#1FF5-040   4 tapes $24.00
#2FF- 040 4 CDs $24.00

Walk with Integrity

#1FF5-1201 4 tapes $24.00
#2FF-1201 4 CDs $24.00

Victory Over Pain

#2FF-002 4 CDs $24.00

Writers Workshop

#WW-002   6 tapes $36.00
#WW-001 6 CDs $36.00

To order, go to **www.arrowbookstore.com**

(see complete resource catalog, current teachings, and conference schedule)

or contact **Arrow Publications, Inc.,** P.O. Box 10102, Cedar Rapids, IA 52410

Phone 1.319.395.7833 or Toll Free 1.877.363.6889   Fax 1.319.395.7353

(VISA/MC/AMERICAN EXPRESS/DISCOVER)

Call for shipping rates and quantity discounts on 10+ books!
Prices subject to change

In Christ's Image Training Materials

Basic Training Manuals

Study series which pulls together four key areas of this ministry: Christlikeness, Humility, Prayer and Unity. Perfect for leadership teams, prayer groups, Bible studies and individuals who are seeking to possess a more Christlike life. It is strongly recommended that these four manuals be read in sequence, as each study is built upon the truths found in the preceding manuals.

#BT-001   set of 4 - retail $48.00

our price $44.00

In Christ's Image Training

Online Correspondence Course

Curriculum developed by
Francis Frangipane

In Christ's Image Training offers four opportunities for enrollment in Level I training each year: January, April, July and October.

Level I: Certification offers four foundational tracks: Christlikeness, Humility, Prayer and Unity. Completion time is six months.

Level II: Leadership Training offers further online teaching by Pastor Francis and other national church leaders. Completion time is three months.

Level III: Facilitation and Commissioning provides spiritual equipping for those preparing for ministerial opportunities.

On-site Impartation and Focused Training offers a three day seminar which can be taken by attendance or via audio tapes. For details watch our website.

Association Graduate students who desire ongoing association with other ICIT graduates, as well as fellowship with other like-minded Christians and churches, are invited to become part of Advancing Church Ministries Association of Churches and Ministries.

In Christ's Image Training center is not a denomination, nor is Advancing Church Ministries (ACM).

Please see our website at www.ICITC.org for enrollment fees and detailed information. 1-319-395-7617, training@inchristsimage.org